So Ghosts Might Stop Composing

poems by

Cheryl Whitehead

Finishing Line Press
Georgetown, Kentucky

So Ghosts Might Stop Composing

This book is dedicated to the memory of Sherdavia Jenkins, and to her mother, Sherrone Jenkins

Copyright © 2019 by Cheryl Whitehead
ISBN 978-1-63534-988-7 First Edition
All rights reserved under International and Pan-American Copyright Conventions. No part of this book may be reproduced in any manner whatsoever without written permission from the publisher, except in the case of brief quotations embodied in critical articles and reviews.

ACKNOWLEDGMENTS

Thank you to the editors of the journals in which the following poems have appeared (sometimes in somewhat different versions or with different titles):

The Southern Poetry Anthology, Volume VII (North Carolina): "The Revivalists"
Mezzo Cammin: "Up in the Air" & "Leningrad Rehab"
Brilliant Corners: A Journal of Jazz and Literature: "Sing, Yes"
Callaloo: "Backwater Blues"

Publisher: Leah Maines
Editor: Christen Kincaid
Cover Art: Richard Taylor
Author Photo: Cheryl Whitehead
Cover Design: Elizabeth Maines McCleavy

Printed in the USA on acid-free paper.
Order online: www.finishinglinepress.com
   also available on amazon.com

Author inquiries and mail orders:
Finishing Line Press
P. O. Box 1626
Georgetown, Kentucky 40324
U. S. A.

Table of Contents

I

The Revivalists 1

Up in the Air 2

Classically Trained 4

Leningrad Rehab 5

Children Running Home from School in Liberty City ... 7

Waking the Elf-King 8

A Kid's Troubles 9

II

Fine & Mellow 12

Dancers in Blue 13

Unkilling Sherdavia 14

Sing, Yes 15

Restless Father 18

A Woman under the Influence 19

III

Late Opus 26

Sixth-Grade Insomniac 27

Backwater Blues 28

Harsh Winds in Liberty City 29

So Ghosts Might Stop Composing 30

Liberty City Lullaby 32

I

THE REVIVALISTS

Ask my family. They'll tell you
I'm a smart aleck, and worse,
educated. Gone to teach in Liberty City
and come back home.
Yes, I'm dangerous,
alone in my house with books
and music around me,
all the places I've seen
clamoring in my memory.
Outside, gunshots echo
at the firing range a quarter mile away.
Changing leaves fidget in the breeze,
and pastures ripen under layers
of dropped chicken manure.
I have a mind to break out of here
like a woman wrongly accused
of thinking only about herself.

Getting what we think we want
causes us trouble. Mama thought
she wanted me home, and I,
craving peace and a slower pace, relented.
Too much about me has changed
and too much about home hasn't.
I sit up at night and will myself not to obsess
about the faces of my young students
whom I couldn't shield from harm.
Beethoven whispers to me "Don't worry."
Dolphy says, "Listen up, mama,
while Trane and me play you a tune."
When I close my eyes, Shostakovich murmurs
"Sleep, dear, being misunderstood
won't endanger your life."

UP IN THE AIR

What else have I got to do but read, watch films,
play horn in the living room for movie stars,
or for flocks of ladybugs who've snuck inside
to hear evening concerts of Unaccompanied Suites?
I'm practicing Bach's Prelude from Suite Six.
Up in the Air comes on TV. George Clooney's
playing a jerk who jets around the country,
firing people. I want to loathe this guy,
but I'm too busy plodding through the Bach,
attempting to fake the double stops. God knows
I'm no Yo-Yo Ma, yet I keep trying
to play the transcribed cello music, using
breath as my bow. When more wrong notes than right ones
hang in the air, frustration causes me
to quit. I take a break and watch the film.
On a business trip, George meets a gorgeous redhead.
They talk in a bar and end up sleeping together.

Raising my horn, I urge him: "Be careful, man."
He doesn't heed my warning. Slowly, I
re-play the lilting 12/8 melody.
Halfway through, I lose my concentration.
There's Clooney smiling, knocking at a door.
His lover answers. She's surprised. Behind her,
children dash upstairs, and a man's voice calls,
"Hey, honey, who's at the door?" I stop playing.

My living room goes dark.
An old scene plays, and in this one, I'm the star.
Palm trees stir in the moonlight. Down the street
from where I've parked, a car alarm goes off.
There, in the passenger seat, the woman I love
uses her hands to wipe my tear-streaked face.
"I'm sorry. I didn't mean for this to happen,"

I whimper, wracked with regret, because I know she's married, yet I want her home with me.
I lift my horn to my mouth, but I can't play.
I close the book of Unaccompanied Suites.

CLASSICALLY TRAINED

In my rearview, I watch Valsean playing
alone on the horizontal bar. Circling in loops,
my sixth-grade student lets one hand go
and swings by the other. Why won't he go home?
I wonder what good I am, the teacher
who uncased her horn on the first day of school
and played *Till Eulenspiegel's Merry Pranks*.
Valsean and his classmates laughed
when I said I'd spent half my life
locked in practice rooms. "You mean
you put your own self in jail?" he said.

Dropping from the bar, Valsean
sprints to scale a ladder before flying
head first down a plastic slide.
On the playground's perimeter,
liquor bottles glint in the sun. I shiver,
though I couldn't possibly fathom
in ten years, I'll find Valsean's picture
in the *Herald*. Under his name
his age will appear, and the time
his body will show in the parlor
at Poitier Funeral Home. That day I'll sit
in my car, leaning my head on the steering wheel.
"Miss W., you too sensitive
to work at this school," Valsean says,
but when I glance up, he's not there.

LENINGRAD REHAB

> *When Shostakovich composed the Fifth, he had begun the sobering sequence of official castigations alternating with 'rehabilitations' he was to experience to the end of his life.*
> —Richard Freed

"My problem is the symphonies I write,"
admitted a man who wore half-inch-thick glasses.
Around the circle, the gathered patients snickered
until a red-haired guard cleared his throat.
The composer rose and crossed the room. He sat
on a stool behind a small upright piano.
"Under normal circumstances," he said,
"you'd hear the strings play slowly, *espressivo*."
Closing his eyes, he fingered the first few bars.
An older gentleman, who never talked,
hummed the tune off-key. "And then the harps
enter like someone walking up the stairs."
A blonde glanced at her stitched-together wrists.
"When the solo flute comes in, the harps begin
to play descending octaves."

                      Leaking through
the room's barred windows, sunshine lit his hands
as he played the *Largo* movement from his Fifth.
When the older man began to weep, a girl
who'd drowned herself in drink took hold of his arm.
The group's sobs drowned out the man's left hand
stretching the notes of the brooding double basses.
Up the keyboard Shostakovich's fingers
reached as he brought the solo oboe in.

Solemnly, doctors stood in doorways and wept.
Janitors exhaled and leaned against
their mops. Their tears dropped into soapy pails.
"In unison, the harp and celesta play
this solo near the end, and then the strings
play *pianissimo* and die away."

The chord expired. Doctors wiped their cheeks
with handkerchiefs as the red-faced guards hovered
near Shostakovich. The sun began to set.
Ice crystals spread on panes.

CHILDREN RUNNING HOME FROM SCHOOL IN LIBERTY CITY
after Donald Justice

September sunlight scorches their path. It burns
Isaiah's cheeks & arms with shadow too bruised
to hide. He runs beside Cedric & Valsean.
They progress, hot-footed, notebooks held in the bend
of their arms, then scatter, crisscrossing littered vacant lots.

Yesterday, Isaiah writhed as his wrists
were twisted behind him & cuffed. His face was wet.
His homework folder had spilled, but his friends
wouldn't bend to gather the loose pages.
They couldn't ignore the drawn Tasers.

Isaiah was flung into a police cruiser's backseat
as I watched from the sidewalk.
Cedric & Valsean didn't dare speak
until the cop car pulled away & headed east
down Northwest Seventy-fifth Street.

Ms. W., we didn't do nothing wrong, Valsean hollered.
We were just walking home, Cedric's voice broke.
As tall as my shoulders, the wiry boys shielded their eyes.
We'd better go tell Isaiah's mother, I said.
A clutch of saw palmettos rustled in the sun.

WAKING THE ELF-KING
In memory of Sherdavia Jenkins

1.

In my night terrors,
your small, wild-eyed mother rides
on horseback with you
draped over the stallion's nape—
your blood wets his auburn mane.

> Inside the belly
> of Maestro Schubert's grand beast
> hide hammers strike strings,
> and the horse's huge black hooves
> pound the misty, rustling ground.

2.

Goethe and Schubert
didn't see death pursuing
a brown girl. *Pop. Pop.*
The shots kick and buck, heat up
the cool, round, black-mouthed barrel.

> Death wears a red cap
> and baggy sweat pants. He flees,
> but cops track him down.
> Men slide a small girl's body
> inside a zippered black bag.

A KID'S TROUBLES
after Randall Jarrell

I'm late to school. Some boys were trying to throw
my book bag in the dumpster, but I grabbed it
and ran. When I finally get to English class,
I disappear in the poem my teacher's reading
about the soldier who's in the field hospital.
Ms. H. is cool, but she can't see how much
I know about that wounded soldier's life,
the things he dreams. Inside my mind, I sit
beside the sleeping soldier and wait for him
to jolt awake, and when he groans I whisper,
"When I get home from school, I stay inside
'cause I can't trust those crazy boys who hang
on the corner, cussing and selling weed. Plus, they
be shooting all the time. And they don't care
that little kids are around here playing. Pow,
pow, pow. That's all those fools know how to do."
Just when I'm feeling good, like I can talk
to the soldier, a man wearing a long white coat
comes by the cot, points out my friend, "Yes, this one."
After the nurse sticks him, he's quiet again.

"Naim, the bell just rang," my teacher says.
I glance up and see the other kids
running out the door, but I don't move.
I'm thinking about the soldier's bandaged eyes.
I'm nervous he's gonna die but ain't no sense
in worrying. There's nothing I can do.
I close my book. Ms. Hartsell's staring at me.
Quick, I grab my stuff. "Later, Ms. H.,"
I tell her and head for second period math.

II

FINE & MELLOW

> *Love will make you do things that you know is wrong.*
> —Billie Holiday

It's Thanksgiving Day.
We've just sat down at my parents' table. Sun
bleeds through the picture window and lights the feast.
Shoveling loads of Mama's fine home cooking
onto our plates, we begin to eat: fried squash,
cornbread, field peas, baked ham, and pumpkin pie.
I'm thinking of my former love far off
in her paradisiacal world: palm trees, sea breezes,
husband and baby girl.

                       My past unwinds
like reels of silent film. The square frames pop
and flicker. There, my love and I sit talking
on a sun-bleached bench. Nearby, an ibis
scavenges, while palm fronds fuss above us.
When she takes my hand, my face burns red.
I want to kiss her, but I don't. I know
her husband! Pulling away, I run to my car.

"Hey! Pass them beets!" my father interrupts.
Breathless, I hand the jar across the table.
Forks clank against my mother's fanciest plates.
Daddy stuffs his mouth. My sister chatters.
She serves herself a second slice of pie.
My ex sits wedged between her man and daughter.
Gathered around, their family laughs. An aunt
takes photographs. When the flash goes off, my ex's
baby crawls across her grandmother's lap.

DANCERS IN BLUE

We tiptoed in like a trio of ballerinas
and held our breath
on the darkened stage of the living room.
Daddy's snoring
imitated a double bass's
dying phrases. We stopped
and stared at his stubbly face.
Over her lips, my mother
placed a finger. *Shhh!* she hissed.
Treading lightly to my room,
I grabbed my horn and headed outside.
As sunlight dimmed,
I climbed in our car's cramped backseat
and played as if in an orchestra pit
where violinists bowed around me,
and clarinetists blew
until their faces burned red.

When dusk's gray curtain fell,
I slipped back into our house
where I heard my father stirring
behind my parents' bedroom door.
Who knew the color of his mood?
My sister and I stayed quiet
while he showered, shaved,
and pulled on his steel-toed boots.
When he left, the storm
door slammed behind him,
and we girls, luckier than Degas'
dancers captured in paint,
twirled wildly through the living room
as Mama, leaning back on the couch,
smiled and clapped her hands.

UNKILLING SHERDAVIA

Twisting its way back out of Sherdavia's throat,
a bullet pops. Her bones and muscles mend.
Her voice box trembles.

Catherine dashes for the porch when the shooting starts.
In the living room, their mother clicks on *The Golden Girls*
and plops on the couch. Out back, where Sherdavia
and Catherine play, two men unpocket their pistols.
Sherdavia undigs a tiny grave and smoothes her baby doll's hair.
"I don't like this game," Catherine complains.

"Why can't you stay in here and play?" their mother asks.
"Please, Mama, can we go outside?"
Early on Saturday morning, the sisters get dressed, wake up.

In their bedroom, a night light glows.
Sherdavia slips into sleep.
Facing each other in bed, the girls chat.
"I don't know. Maybe we can ride our bikes," Sherdavia answers.
"What are we gonna do tomorrow?" Catherine asks.
The sisters crawl under their sheet. Miss Lion
meows and jumps between their feet.

SING, YES

I. LATE QUARTET

Walking my family's homestead,
I saw my grandfather standing
by the pasture gate. He waved
to welcome me home,
then disappeared from wherever he came—
his visit was like hearing
Beethoven's *Heiliger Dankgesang:*
the composer's convalescent breath
filling the old man's spirit
like leaves in dead wind.

II. BALLAD

Sometimes I miss the Florida sun,
and the banana tree flapping
its flimsy fan-like leaves
in her backyard. How long does it take
to fall for love, and then forget her?
Is it wrong to say I want to sleep
next to a woman, brown and lovely
to the touch—her body singing
as sweet as Coltrane and Dolphy
playing strains of *Naima*
on a back-lit stage?

III. PASTORAL

Around my family's land,
there's a fence of cedar posts
that Granddaddy and Daddy cut.

When I was a girl, I rode with them
to the woods, and with a hatchet,
whacked a felled trunk. By the creek,
the three of us worked, white breath
slipping out of our mouths,
while water bubbled over ice and rocks
near an old junk pile. *It's a might cold,*
Granddaddy said before we threw the axes
and leftover barbed wire onto the lift
behind the tractor. Though Granddaddy's
ten years buried, the fence we built
still keeps the cows in. The fence,
yes, it and the melody, outlast a man.

IV. IMPRESSIONS

On the nights I'm loneliest, I listen
to Coltrane and Dolphy playing
a concert in Copenhagen with Jones,
Workman and Tyner. After a false start,
Trane speaks to the audience. *Thank you very kindly,
ladies and gentlemen,* he says. The South
pours over the stage floor like a river cresting its banks.
When the applause stops, he starts to play—
slightly arching his back, he looms, tall,
wide-bodied, tenor in his hands.
Through that horn, he calls to Eric D.,
who answers him note for note on alto,
the knot on his forehead bulging like a root
pushing at muddy ground.

V. HYMN

Granddaddy and his kin arranged
their piles of junk on the creek's slope
as if to sing, *yes, we was here.* Atop
a mound of old wash tubs, Daddy's first trike
sits rusting. Barbed wire and briars
loop over the handlebars. On evenings I go
to their place to hike, Daddy naps in his chair.
Mama solves the daily crossword. One day
I know they'll leave me alone in the world.
I'll walk with their spirit remnants following me,
their voices humming, "Daughter, we're making
a place for you where we are now."

VI. ERRATA

My mind aches with regret when I think of how
my imagination fashioned an alternate ending
for she and I (a house, our children),
constructed a life that could never go beyond
the mind of the lover in which it was born,
like one of Beethoven's failed melodies
written before he thought of something better
and angrily scratched the erring notes away.

RESTLESS FATHER

i.
Don't smoke or drink, eat less, the doctor told him
but that advice, reiterated by his wife,
turns Daddy as ornery as the ass
that guards the calves behind the neighbor's
noisy chicken houses.

ii.
When he and Mama were young,
they'd lock their bedroom door at eight p.m.
Under the jamb would come the muted cries
and then, the whine of water humming in pipes.
Afterwards, he'd sit on the toilet lid
as she dried his hair. At ten p.m., he'd slide
his feet into steel-toed boots and leave for the mill.

iii.
Now he sleeps upstairs. Mama beds down
in the master bedroom. All night he rolls
and pulls tucked sheets from under mattress corners.
He can't say what causes the fitfulness
between his dreams, but he knows he doesn't care
to lie beside her and watch the moonlight
glisten in her graying hair.

iv.
Only at dusk, when he sits alone on the porch,
smoking Old Golds and petting his Lab,
does he get a fleeting feeling
that he should give a damn. He watches fireflies
blink, go out. Before he goes in the house, he drops
a half-smoked cigarette in his bourbon glass.

A WOMAN UNDER THE INFLUENCE

> *It just seems to me that women are alone and they are made prisoner by their own love. If they commit to something then they have committed to it and it's torture.*
> —John Cassavetes

It's 3:15. Mother's in the street,
jumping up & down. "My sweethearts
are on that bus!" she yells. People sharing
the sidewalk stare. "What're you looking at?"
she spits & flicks her wrist.

The bus pulls up. Her older son jumps off.
"Hi, Mom." Hugging him tight, she spins around.
Her girl & brown-eyed boy hop down.
"Hi, sweethearts! How was school?"

The four of them jog home.
They sit together on the porch.
Catching her breath, Mother asks,
"When you think of me, do you think
Mommy's dopey or strange?"

"No," her older son says. "I think
you're pretty   smart   nervous."

"Thank you, honey!" she hugs his neck.

Mother wants to make some fun
for after school by hanging pink
& blue balloons. Her children twirl.
As she eggs them on, she sings
Swan Lake with the radio
& pirouettes around the lawn.

Look at babies! My beautiful swans!

After he's spent the night
repairing busted city water pipes,
her husband's home. He's brought
his hungry crew along. They greet
his wife. Meekly, Mother stands
in the dining room. She smoothes
her light blonde hair.

Oh, god. Why did he bring them here?

"Hello, hello." She shakes their hands. "Spaghetti?" she asks.

"Yes," they smile.

At breakfast they have a toast.
As they drink red wine & eat,
a brown man sings *Aida*. Mother stands.
"Dance with me, handsome." She spins
behind his back. Stopping mid-phrase,
the crewman looks down. When she touches
his shoulder, Daddy blows his top,
"Sit your ass down!"

Stoically, the men file out. "Thank you,"
they say, & when they've gone away,
"You're wacko!" her husband yells.

I didn't ask you to bring them here.
Why can't it just be us? Just us.

That evening Mother cuts her wrist.
When Daddy wrestles the blade away,
she escapes & climbs on the couch.
Twirling & singing *Swan Lake*,
she twists her bloody wrist.

"Get off the couch, or I'll knock you down!"
Around Daddy's legs, the children swirl.
They scream & push him back.

Dah—dah, dah, dah, dah,
dah—dah, dah. Oh, how much
I love to dance. I'm the swan,
not Mother. Mother's gone away.

After Daddy doctors her wrist,
they put their kids to bed.
Mother kisses three belly buttons.
"Love you, banana," she says.
"Love you, too," her younger son exhales.

"Love you, banana," she says.
"Love you, too," her older son whispers.

"Love you, banana," she says.
"Love you, Mommy," her daughter yawns
before she kisses the tip of her mommy's nose
& then re-puckers to peck her lips.

> *Okay. Okay. I'm A-Okay.*
> *The kids are safe. I'm okay.*
> *Oh, how I wish I could dance.*

The next day, it's Daddy who gets
the children out of bed & fed.
"Where's Mommy?"

It's Daddy who gets
the children bathed & dressed.
"Where's Mommy?"

It's he who takes
the kids to school,
& drives to work.

The morning sun exposes
steep slopes of a granite pit
where he & his whispering men
walk behind a six-wheeled Caterpillar.
"Don't discuss my wife!" he screams.

Gears   ropes   Daddy's fear.
Shovels   gloves   Daddy's love.
Hard hats   rocks   Daddy's rage.

———————————————

He's edgy & wants to see his kids.
Leaving work early with a crewman friend,
he drives a red construction truck to school.
When the kids come out, "We're going
to the beach," he says as he lifts them in.

At the beach: rocks   waves
white swim trunks with yellow trim.
Hairy hamstrings adorn the shore.
Daddy's fussy. He can't relax.

On the way back home, the kids
share his beer. "Not too much," he says.

"Just a sip," he adds. "I'm sorry
Mommy had to go away."

After his crewman drops them off,
he puts sad & tipsy bananas to bed.

———————————————

Six months later, he's planned
her homecoming party. The house is full
of family, friends. "Are you crazy?" Grandma asks.
"What party? Only the family!" she yells.

Walking out in the rain, he glances
down the street. When he comes back in,
he tells the guests to leave. By the door he stands
& shakes each person's hand.

Mother arrives in a beige sedan.
It's raining hard. Her hair gets wet.
Quiet & scared, she walks toward the house.
A brown barrette sparkles in her hair.
In the living room, she sees her husband, who apologizes.
"I've got to see the children," Mother whispers
as she opens two sliding doors.
"Did you miss us, Mommy?" they glance up & ask.
Her forehead crinkles. "No emotions, now," she says.

My babies. Their perfect faces.
Do they think I meant to leave them here?

That night, the parents put their kids to bed.
"Good night, Mommy."

"Good night, bananas. I love you." Mommy tucks them in.
Daddy turns off the light.

III

LATE OPUS

Clouds pack thunder. Rain.
Beethoven's *Grosse Fuge*
blasts from my speakers.

I drive on. Four men
wielding bows unspool flurries
of discordant tones.

Gray skies sag and smoke
billows from the cigarette
factory's smoke stacks.

Ahead, brake lights blink.
A green street sweeper's big brooms
brush and spin against

the curb. Carrying
bags with lunches packed inside,
a clutch of school kids

cross the railroad tracks
to the beat of a deaf man's
polyphonic dreams.

SIXTH-GRADE INSOMNIAC

1.

Over Isaiah's bed the glow of streetlights
sneaks in. His curtains drift as he eavesdrops
on the boys next door. "Hey, pass that over here,"
he hears a deep voice say, followed by coughs
and low-pitched laughs. Isaiah loves their talk.
Their voices are a black blanket wrapping up
the cold inside his head. *Pop-pop-pop-pop!*
Gunshots slice the air. Isaiah rolls onto the floor.
"Shit!" he hears a familiar voice and footsteps
running away.

2.

"I don't know why he sleeps at school,"
Isaiah's mother tells his teacher.
Isaiah cries. "Talk, son. Tell this lady
what's wrong." Isaiah leans back.
His eyes snap shut. He feels the mango-
sweet breeze against his skin.

3.

Isaiah writes his name on his spelling test.
M-I-S-T-E-R D-A-R-K-N-E-S-S.
He listens to his teacher call out words
like *orbit, trajectory, velocity.*
Floating around his head, the letters hum
like honey bees near his ears and speak
their names real soft and sweet to him. I-am-
Mister-Darkness, I-am-Mister-Darkness,
I-am-Mister-Darkness, he writes
until his notebook paper is
the starless black cape of night.

BACKWATER BLUES
>*Then trouble's taking place in the lowlands at night.*
>—Bessie Smith

What you mean they killed him?
  Cedric's brown eyes flicker.
I'm not sure what to say.
  My students stare at me in disbelief,
half-expecting that I might bring young Emmett back,
  change his story to one that doesn't end
with his tortured, teenage body dragging
  the Tallahatchie's rocky river bottom.

No one could be that cruel, Iris, the child,
  in the back of the class whispers.
This morning she stopped me in the hall
  to say last night she heard
in the flat above hers, a man
  slapping his wife.
I imagined the screams. The sirens.
  The policemen's feet
striking each step like the hammers
  inside a piano's growling belly.

I put on a song
  and tell the kids: Listen for the Blues
trumpeter turning his bell
  into a woman's wide open throat,
hear him making a picture of her
  mired up to her black-stockinged ankles
in red clay muck.

  My students tilt their heads
as mouthfuls of misery head straight through
  the trumpet's brass tubing and spill
into the honey-thick air. Bessie tells them,
  When it thunder and lightnin' and the wind begin to blow,
  When it thunder and lightnin' and the wind begin to blow,
  there's thousands of people ain't got no place to go.

HARSH WINDS IN LIBERTY CITY
after a line from César Vallejo
for Sherdavia Jenkins

They don't know why harsh winds whistle in my poems
or ruffle God's hair when He looks down on Liberty Square,
a robe spilling over His knees & pooling like milk
on the apartment building's roof. They don't know why

God drinks a glass of sweet tea while leaning back
on a throne of sunlight, or why palm fronds clatter on
with their percussive speech. They don't know why
a clot of green parakeets squawks a prophesy, & no one

listens, so the flock flies off. A thunderstorm can send
the children in. God has that power. Instead, boys & girls
tear through the square. Spokes glitter, while Grandmas
pin wash to the lines. They don't know why a man strolls out

on his porch & lights up the courtyard with automatic rounds
as his intended target slips behind a building & disappears.
They don't know why the children scatter. Except for one.
A girl of nine years & fifty-seven pounds, lying face down,

half in her house—half out. On the day Sherdavia died,
her pink sneakers & sundress dried on the line. Police tape
trembled. I don't know why God kept the rain tucked
in his robe pocket, or why sunshine flooded the square.

SO GHOSTS MIGHT STOP COMPOSING

I   A GIRL UNCONVINCED

On Sundays, I waited for the blue church bus
to pick me up and whisk me across our city.
What kept me riding was not so much my faith
but what I could win if I showed up enough
to please the Baptist brethren. In week sixteen
I won a radio for perfect church attendance.
The small black box with silver antennae sang
to me at night while in all His great goodness,
God never made a peep. No, nothing. Nada.
No voice, no gust of wind to send along
a message: *Hello. Hello. It's me. I'm here.*

II   THE CHURCH PIANIST

She played with power, electric belief
in something higher. Every Sunday she sang
A Bridge over Troubled Water for us, the kids
transported there from the other side of town.
When she leaned into the keys, her blond hair
brushed her cheeks, and she nodded, our cue
to join her on the song's chorus. I studied the kids
whose hopeful faces gleamed. Did they believe?

III   ROOKIE TEACHER

When my students showed up for school,
an awful sorrow flickered in their eyes.
Brashly, they walked the halls
with balled-up fists and hid their fears

of what could happen any night
in Liberty Square. Closed in by fences
topped with razor wire, the neighborhood
was alien to me as were the stained sidewalks
and helicopters churning the sky.

IV   TWENTY YEARS AFTER THE BLACK TRANSISTOR

Maybe my lack of faith doomed my students,
or maybe it was a universal law embedded
in starry particles that prompted God
never to interfere with humans or their doings.
It doesn't matter now. The graves are dug,
the coffins filled. Tomorrow, a frightened mother
will rush outside to find her daughter bleeding
and trying to breathe. Hearing the woman's screams,
the neighbors will run to form a trembling fort
around the girl lying crumpled on her porch.
In class we'll stare at Sherdavia's empty chair.

V   THE BORN SKEPTIC

All the church people wanted was to win
me over, to free me from the world of sin.
Being skeptical and full of questions,
I had no patience for their bland evasions.
I left the church at the tender age of ten.
Now more than halfway through my life, I still
sleep late on Sundays. In my dreams,
ghosts crowd around me, closing me in.

LIBERTY CITY LULLABY

I fear coiled razor wire
I fear the streets on fire
I fear the sun & rain
I fear the daytime train

I fear the liquor stores
I fear barred windows & doors
I fear bail bondsmen's shops
I fear stray bullets & cops

I fear yellow caution tape
I fear a shooter's escape
I fear police helicopters
& tired trauma room doctors

I fear teddy bear shrines
& *Stop the Violence* signs
I fear the gaping ground
& a small coffin going down

I fear the blown streetlights
I fear the *Bill of Rights*
I fear *The First 48*
& the verdict coming late

I fear the vacant lot
I fear the dumpster's rot
I fear the ice cream truck
& its song of bad luck

Hush, hush little child
Your dreams have grown wild
Hush, don't you cry
Lulla, Lullaby

ADDITIONAL ACKNOWLEDGEMENTS

I would like to thank Charles Martin, Diane Thiel, Mary Jo Salter and Marilyn Nelson who provided guidance on many poems in this book. Thank you to manuscript consultant, Charlie Bondhus, and to Lolita Stewart-White, Addy McCulloch, Stephanie Queen and friends in the Sewanee School of Letters, the Sewanee Writers' Conference and The Fine Arts Work Center who helped me to hone these poems.

This book is dedicated to the memory of Sherdavia Jenkins, (March 22, 1997-July 1, 2006) and to her mother, Sherrone Jenkins (November 4, 1968-October 7, 2018).

Sherdavia was a straight-A student, chess champion, gifted artist and ebullient child who had boundless enthusiasm for learning and life. I often wonder what she would have accomplished in her adult life. Sherrone Jenkins was a staunch advocate for her children, and the picture that remains in my mind is of her sitting in the school library with Sherdavia and her siblings, reading to them and helping them with their homework. She and I remained friends until she passed away on October 7, 2018.

Cheryl Whitehead is a writer, musician and cinematographer who lives in North Carolina. Her poems have appeared in *The Southern Poetry Anthology, Crab Orchard Review, Callaloo, Measure, The Hopkins Review*, and other journals. She has been the recipient of grants and scholarships from the Sewanee Writers' Conference, the North Carolina Writers' Network, Tigertail, and the Astraea Foundation. Whitehead has written about visual art for *Milieu Magazine*, and her cinematography work has shown at the Museum of Contemporary Art in Miami, the Pan-African Film Festival in Los Angeles, the Langston Hughes African-American Film Festival in Seattle, and the Leeds Underground Film Festival in the United Kingdom.

She is also a horn player who has taught music at Carthage College in Kenosha, Wisconsin, and in public schools in Greensboro, North Carolina and Miami, Florida, where she began a partnership between the students of Lillie C. Evans Elementary School and the musicians of The New World Symphony. Whitehead invited National Book Award Finalist and Kingsley Tufts Poetry Award Winner, Patricia Smith, to conduct poetry workshops and community poetry events with the students at Lillie C. Evans.

Whitehead received her Master of Fine Arts in Poetry from the Sewanee School of Letters, where she studied with Charles Martin, Diane Thiel, and Andrew Hudgins. Currently, she teaches English at the Middle College at North Carolina A&T State University, an all-male, college-preparatory academy affiliated with the Guilford County Schools.